Alfred's Basic Piano Library

Prep Course
FOR THE YOUNG BEGINNER

Activity & Ear Training Book • Level A

Gayle Kowalchyk • E. L. Lancaster

A delightful coloring workbook filled with a variety of fun activities,
the material reinforces musical concepts and includes well-planned listening activities
that develop ear-training skills.

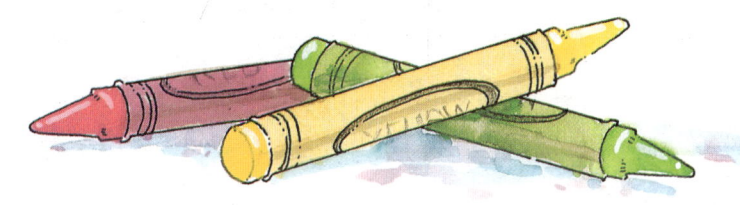

Layout by Linda Lusk **Illustrations by Christine Finn** **Art Direction by Ted Engelbart**

Alfred

© Copyright MCMLXXXIX by Alfred Publishing Co., Inc.
All rights reserved.   Printed in USA.

Instructions for Use

1. This ACTIVITY & EAR TRAINING BOOK is designed to be used with Alfred's PREP COURSE for the young beginner, LESSON BOOK A.

2. This book is coordinated page-by-page with the LESSON BOOK, and assignments are ideally made according to the instructions in the upper right corner of each page of the ACTIVITY & EAR TRAINING BOOK.

3. Many students enjoy completing these pages so much that they will want to go beyond the assigned material. However, it is best to wait until the indicated pages in the LESSON BOOK have been covered before the corresponding material in this book is studied.

4. This ACTIVITY & EAR TRAINING BOOK reinforces each concept presented in the LESSON BOOK through carefully designed pages for young children to color. It also specifically focuses on the training and development of the ear.

5. Listening examples on certain pages (5, 10, 11, 14, 15, 16, 18, 20, 22, 24, 26, 28, 31, 32, 36, 40, 43) are best completed at the lesson. Examples for these pages are given for the teacher (pages 45–48). All other pages may be assigned for home study if so desired.

Left Hand and Right Hand

1. Color the LEFT HAND **red.**
2. Color the RIGHT HAND **blue.**

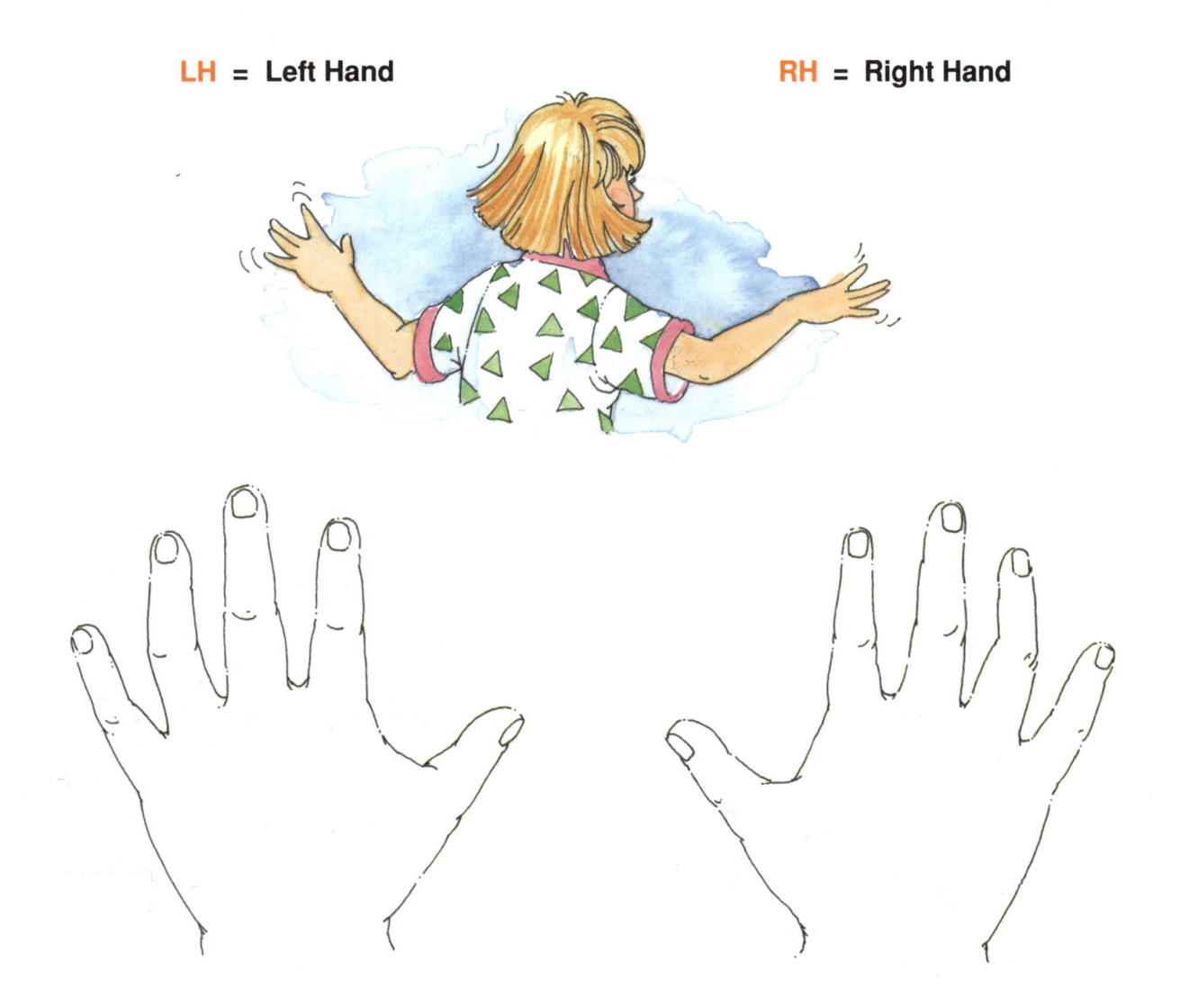

Use with Alfred's Basic Piano Library
PREP COURSE, Lesson Book A, page 5.

LH = **Left Hand**   **RH** = **Right Hand**

Use with page 5.

Finger Numbers

1. Color LH & RH fingers 1 **purple.**
2. Color LH & RH fingers 2 **pink.**
3. Color LH & RH fingers 3 **green.**
4. Color LH & RH fingers 4 **blue.**
5. Color LH & RH fingers 5 **red.**

LH
Left Hand

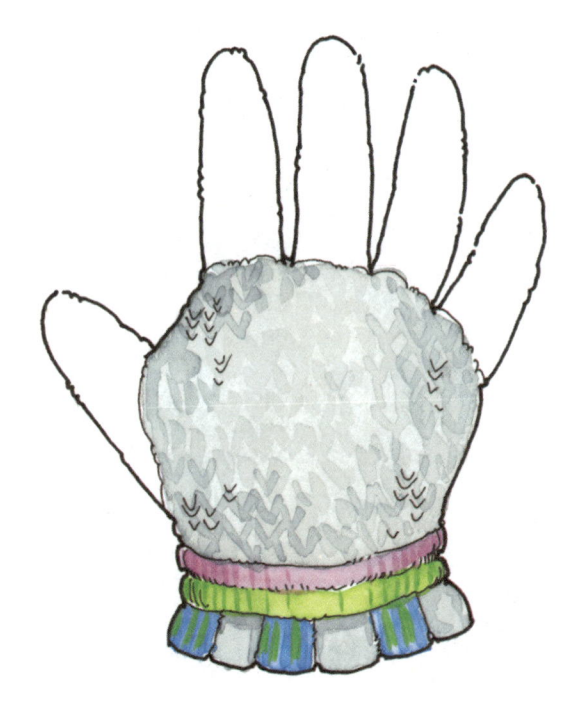

RH
Right Hand

High and Low

Your teacher will play HIGH and LOW sounds.

- Circle the MOUSE if you hear a HIGH sound.
- Circle the ELEPHANT if you hear a LOW sound.

Use with page 6.

1.

2.

3.

4.

TEACHER: See page 45.

Use with page 7.

2 Black Keys and 3 Black Keys

1. Circle all of the 2 BLACK-KEY groups in **red**.
2. Circle all of the 3 BLACK-KEY groups in **blue**.

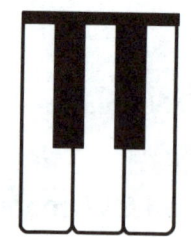

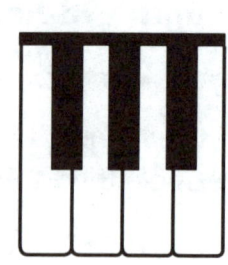

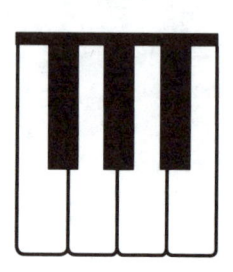

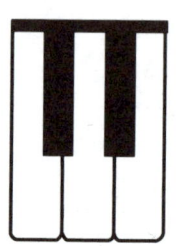

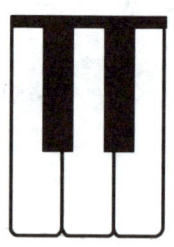

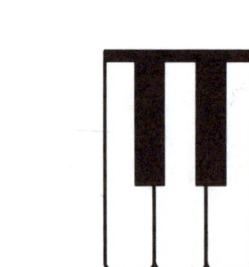

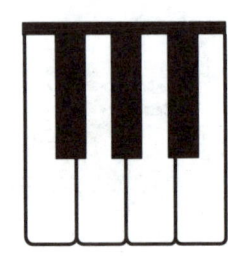

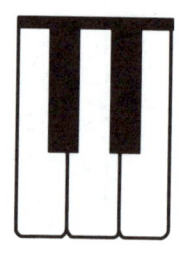

Quarter Note

1. Color the areas containing a QUARTER NOTE (♩) **brown**.
2. Color the areas containing a 2 BLACK-KEY GROUP **blue**.
3. Color the areas containing a 3 BLACK-KEY GROUP **green**.

8

Use with page 8.

Left Hand

1. Color finger 2 **pink** on each LEFT HAND.
2. Color finger 3 **green** on each LEFT HAND.

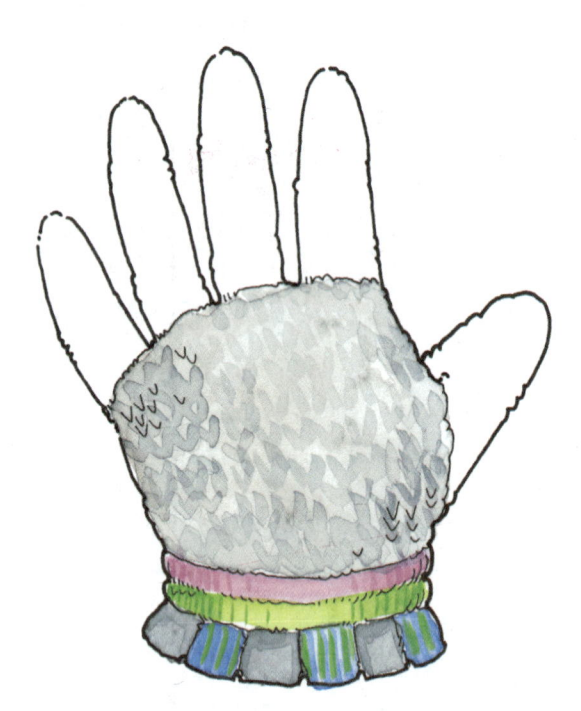

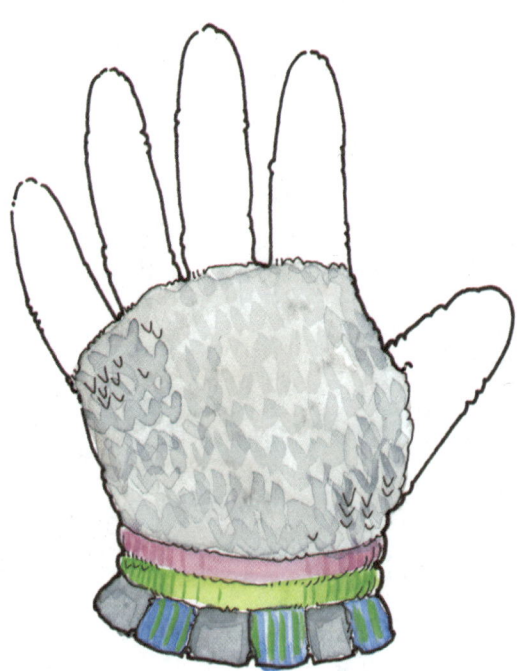

Right Hand

1. Color finger 2 **pink** on each RIGHT HAND.
2. Color finger 3 **green** on each RIGHT HAND.

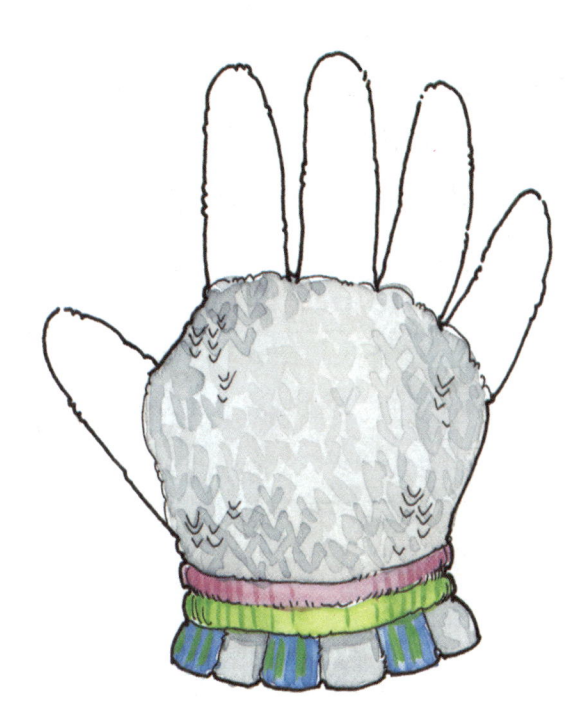

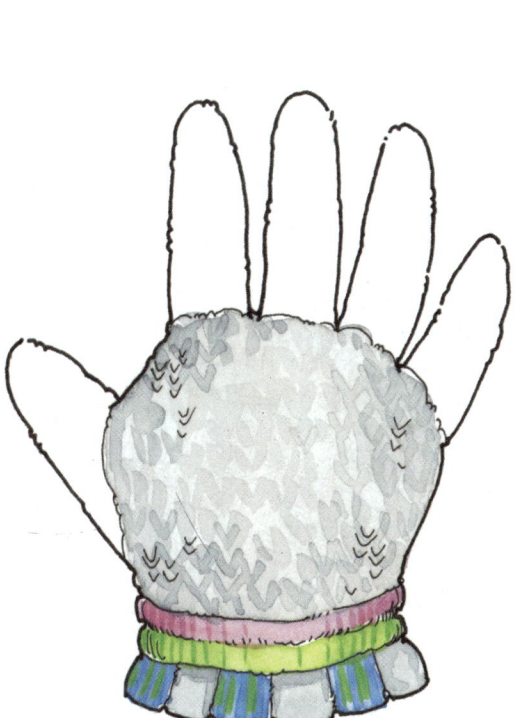

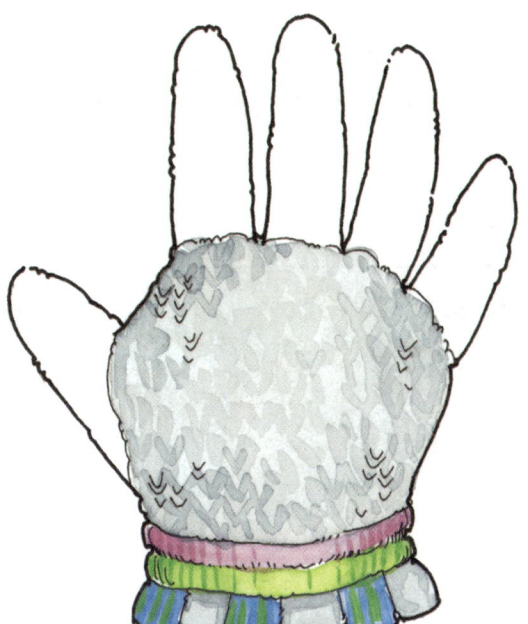

Quarter and Half Notes

Your teacher will clap a rhythm pattern.
Circle the pattern that you hear.

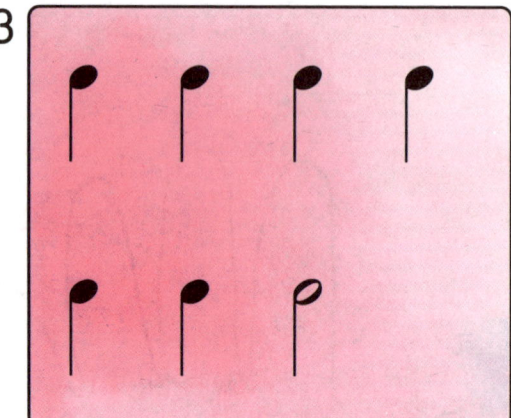

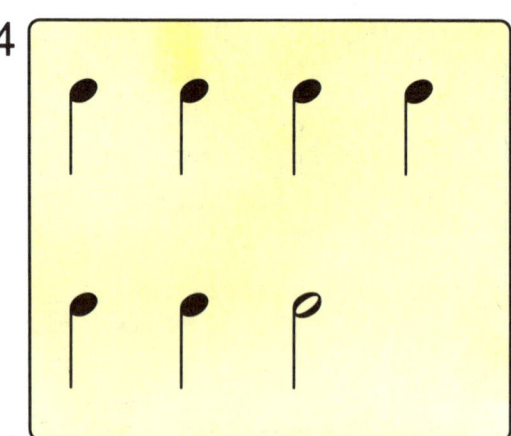

Use with page 10.

TEACHER: See page 45.

Up and Down

Your teacher will play sounds that go UP or DOWN.

- Color the airplane TAKING OFF if the sounds go UP. Choose any color.
- Color the airplane LANDING if the sounds go DOWN. Choose any color.

1.

2.

3.

4.

TEACHER: See page 45.

Quarter and Half Notes

1. Color the areas containing QUARTER NOTES (♩) **red**.
2. Color the areas containing HALF NOTES (♪) **blue**.

Use with page 12.

Quarter, Half and Whole Notes

1. Draw a **pink** circle around each QUARTER (♩) note. Make the circle touch the string.
2. Draw a **purple** circle around each HALF (♩) note. Make the circle touch the string.
3. Draw a **green** circle around each WHOLE (o) note. Make the circle touch the string.

14

Use with page 14.

Piano and Forte

Your teacher will play SOFT and LOUD sounds.

- Circle the f if you hear LOUD sounds.
- Circle the p if you hear SOFT sounds.

1.

2.

3.

4.

TEACHER: See page 45

Quarter, Half and Whole Notes

Your teacher will clap a rhythm pattern.
Circle the pattern that you hear.

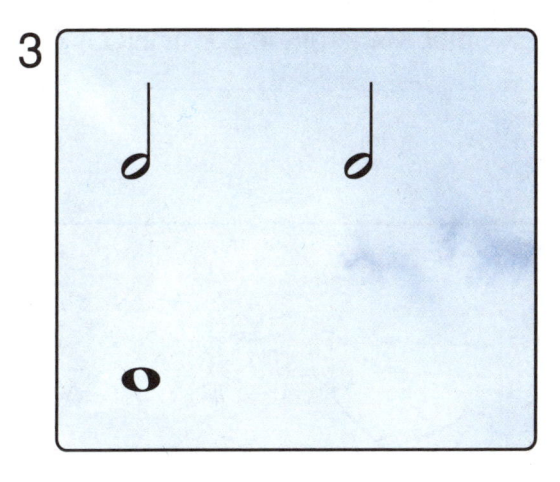

16

Use with page 16.

Musical Alphabet

Your teacher will play the letters of the MUSICAL ALPHABET going UP or DOWN.

- Color the airplane TAKING OFF if the alphabet goes UP. Choose any color.
- Color the airplane LANDING if the alphabet goes DOWN. Choose any color.

1

2

3

4

TEACHER: See page 46.

White Keys A-B-C

1. Color each A **red**.
2. Color each B **blue**.
3. Color each C **yellow**.

A

B

C

High and Low

Your teacher will play A-B-C groups HIGH or LOW on the keyboard.

- Circle the HIGH A-B-C group if the sounds are HIGH.
- Circle the LOW A-B-C group if the sounds are LOW.

Use with page 18.

1

2

TEACHER: See page 46.

19

Use with page 19.

White Keys C-D-E

1. Color each C **yellow.**
2. Color each D **brown.**
3. Color each E **purple.**

Up and Down

Use with pages 20–21.

Your teacher will play patterns that go UP or DOWN in the MIDDLE C POSITION. Circle the pattern that you hear.

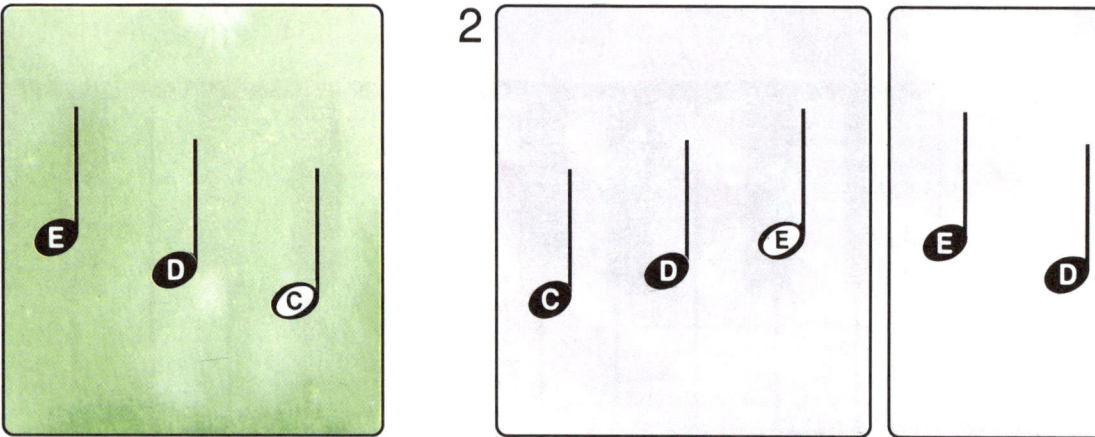

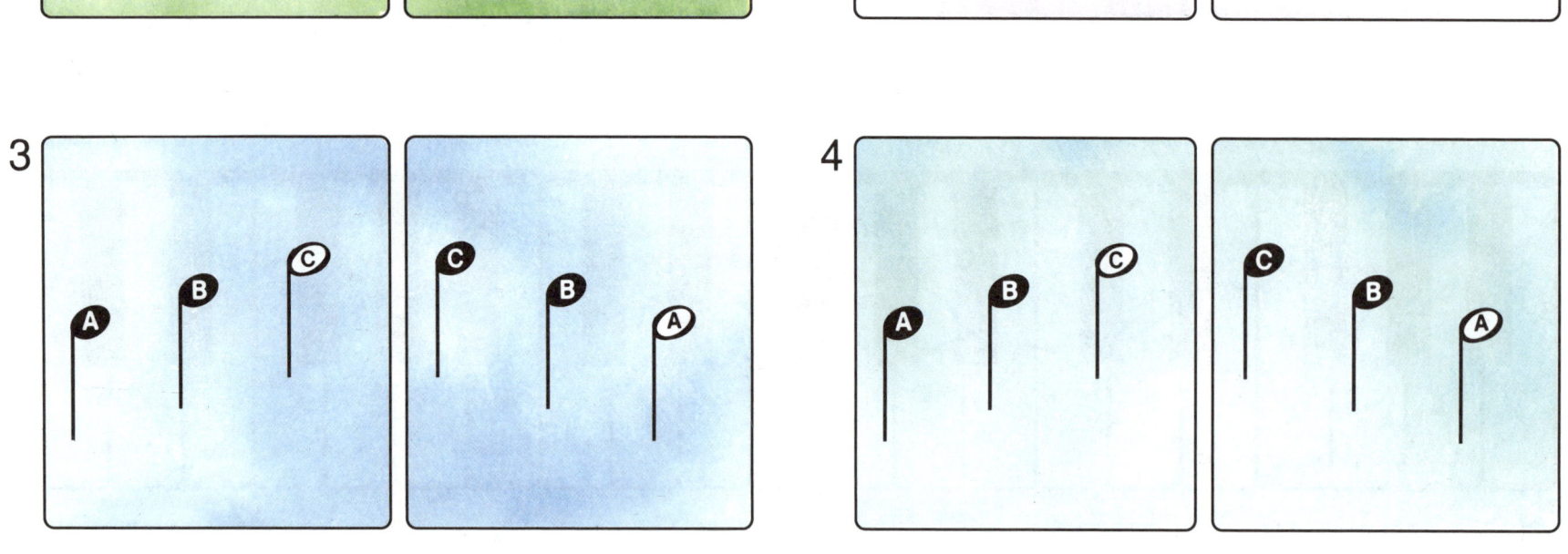

1. C D E | E D C

2. C D E | E D C

3. A B C | C B A

4. A B C | C B A

TEACHER: See page 46.

White Keys F-G

- Color each F **green.**
- Color each G **pink.**

22

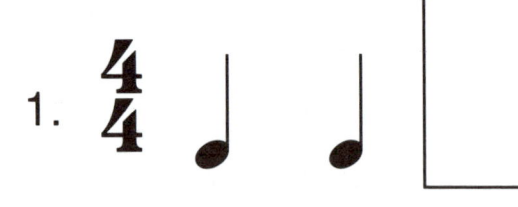

Use with page 23.

Quarter and Half Notes

Your teacher will clap a rhythm pattern using QUARTER and HALF notes.

Draw the missing note (♩ or ♪) in the box.

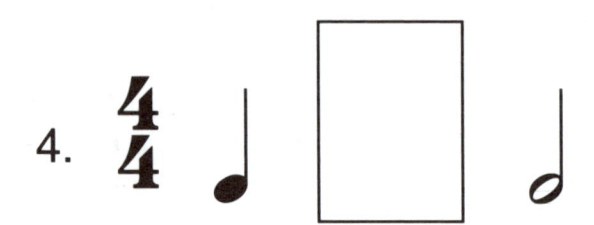

TEACHER: See page 46.

Middle C Position

1. Color MIDDLE C's **yellow.**
2. Color the remaining RIGHT HAND POSITION keys **blue.**
3. Color the remaining LEFT HAND POSITION keys **red.**
4. Write each KEY NAME below.

RH

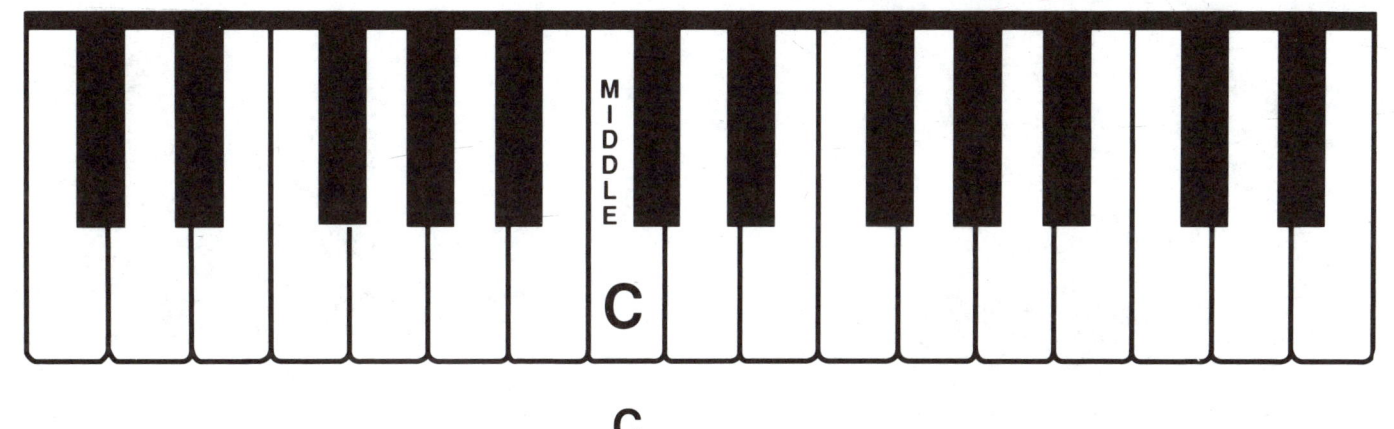

C _ _ _ _

LH

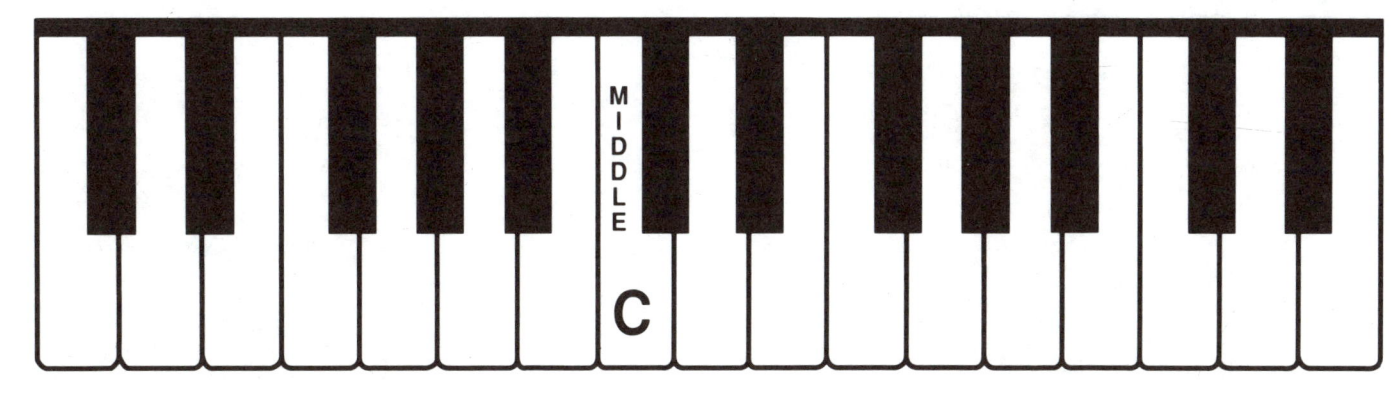

_ _ _ _ C

24

Use with page 25.

Mezzo Forte and Forte

Your teacher will play MODERATELY LOUD and LOUD sounds.

- Circle the *mf* if you hear MODERATELY LOUD sounds.
- Circle the *f* if you hear LOUD sounds.

1.

2.

3.

4.

TEACHER: See page 47.

C Position

1. Color the RIGHT HAND C POSITION keys **blue**.
2. Color the LEFT HAND C POSITION keys **red**.
3. Write each KEY NAME below.

RH

MIDDLE **C**

C _ _ _ _

LH

MIDDLE **C**

_ _ _ _ _

Quarter, Half and Whole Notes

Your teacher will clap a rhythm pattern.
Circle the pattern that you hear.

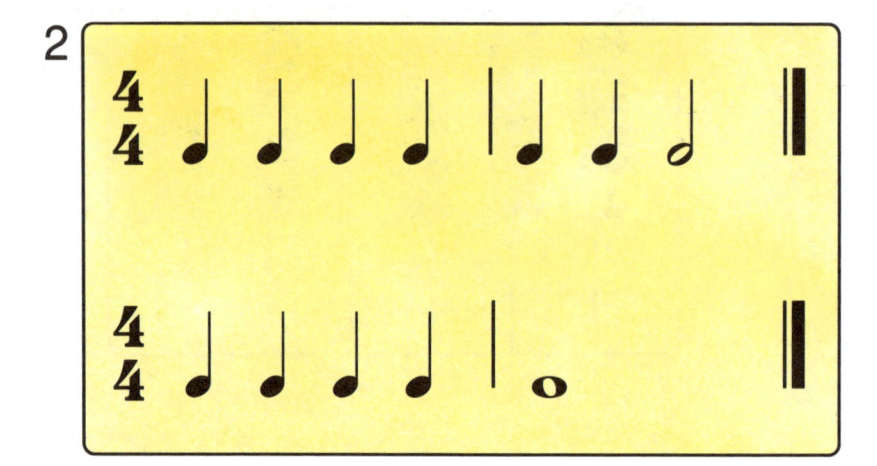

Use with page 27.

TEACHER: See page 47.

Quarter, Half, Dotted Half and Whole Notes

1. Color the areas containing QUARTER NOTES (♩) **blue**.
2. Color the areas containing HALF NOTES (𝅗𝅥) **green**.
3. Color the areas containing DOTTED HALF NOTES (𝅗𝅥.) **red**.
4. Color the areas containing WHOLE NOTES (o) **yellow**.

Use with pages 28–29.

Quarter, Half and Dotted Half Notes

Your teacher will clap a rhythm pattern.
Circle the pattern that you hear.

1.
- 3/4 ♩ ♩ ♩ | ♩. ‖
- 3/4 ♩ ♩ | ♩. ‖

2. 
- 3/4 ♩ ♩ ♩ 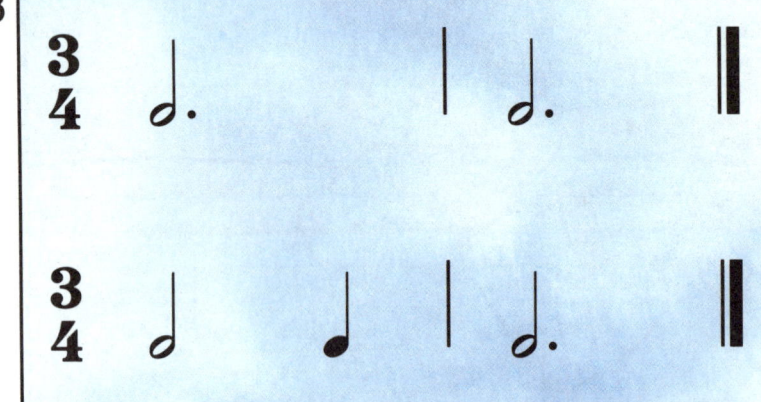 | ♩ ‖
- 3/4 ♩ ♩ | ♩. ‖

3.
- 3/4 ♩. | ♩. ‖
- 3/4 ♩ ♩ | ♩. ‖

4.
- 3/4 ♩. | ♩. ‖
- 3/4 ♩ ♩ ♩ | ♩. ‖

Line and Space Notes

- Color each LINE note **red.**
- Color each SPACE note **blue.**

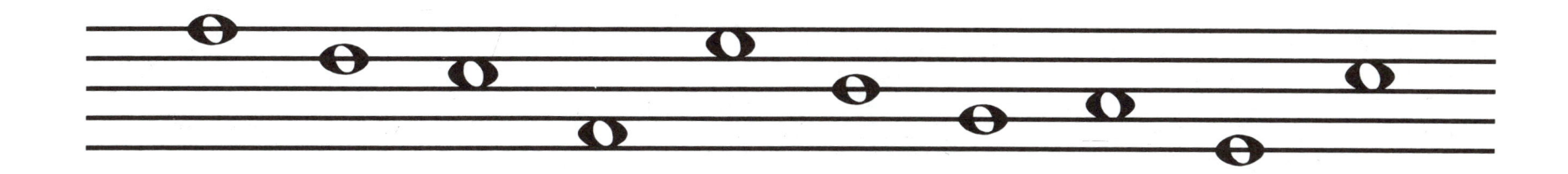

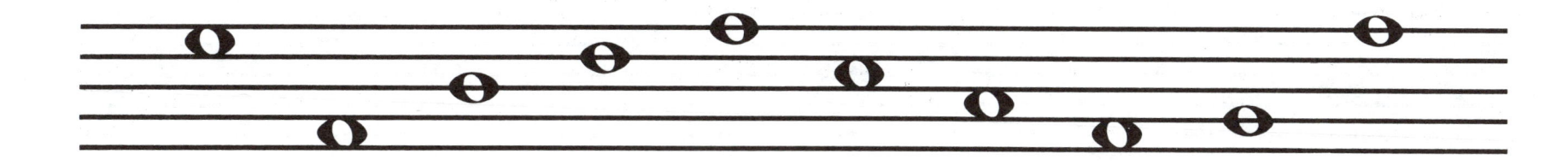

Bass Clef F

Color each bass clef F **black.**

Use with page 32.

31

Use with page 33.

Piano and Mezzo Forte

Your teacher will play SOFT and MODERATELY LOUD sounds.

- Circle the *p* if you hear SOFT sounds.
- Circle the *mf* if you hear MODERATELY LOUD sounds.

1.

2.

3.

4.

TEACHER: See page 47.

Quarter, Half, Dotted Half and Whole Notes

Your teacher will clap a rhythm pattern.
Circle the pattern that you hear.

Use with page 34.

1.
4/4 ♩ ♩ ♩ ♩ ‖
4/4 ♩ ♩ ♩ ♩ ‖

2.
3/4 ♩ ♩ | ♩. ‖
3/4 ♩ ♩ ♩ | ♩. ‖

3.
4/4 ♩ ♩ ‖
4/4 ♩ ♩ ♩ ‖

4.
3/4 ♩ ♩ | ♩. ‖
3/4 ♩. | ♩. ‖

TEACHER: See page 48.

Bass Clef C Position

1. Color the areas containing a C **gray.**
2. Color the areas containing a D **yellow.**
3. Color the areas containing an E **blue.**
4. Color the areas containing an F **green.**
5. Color the areas containing a G **pink.**

Treble Clef G

Color each treble clef G **red**.

Use with page 36.

35

Use with page 37.

Treble and Bass Clefs

1. Color the areas containing a TREBLE CLEF **green.**
2. Color the areas containing a BASS CLEF **orange.**

Use with page 38.

Up and Down

Your teacher will play patterns that go UP or DOWN in C POSITION. Circle the pattern that you hear.

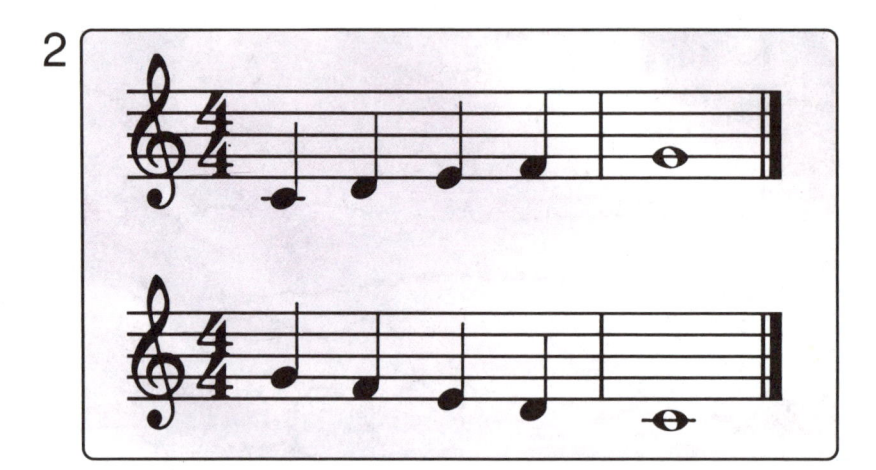

TEACHER: See page 48.

Treble Clef C Position

1. Color the areas containing a C **green.**
2. Color the areas containing a D **brown.**
3. Color the areas containing an E **pink.**
4. Color the areas containing an F **purple.**
5. Color the areas containing a G **blue.**

The Grand Staff

1. Trace the TREBLE CLEF in **red**.
2. Trace the BASS CLEF in **blue**.
3. Trace the BRACE and BAR LINES in **black**.
4. Color the LINE NOTES **yellow**.
5. Color the SPACE NOTES **orange**.

Use with page 40.

C Position on the Grand Staff

1. Color each C on the GRAND STAFF and KEYBOARD **yellow**.
2. Color each D on the GRAND STAFF and KEYBOARD **brown**.
3. Color each E on the GRAND STAFF and KEYBOARD **purple**.
4. Color each F on the GRAND STAFF and KEYBOARD **green**.
5. Color each G on the GRAND STAFF and KEYBOARD **pink**.

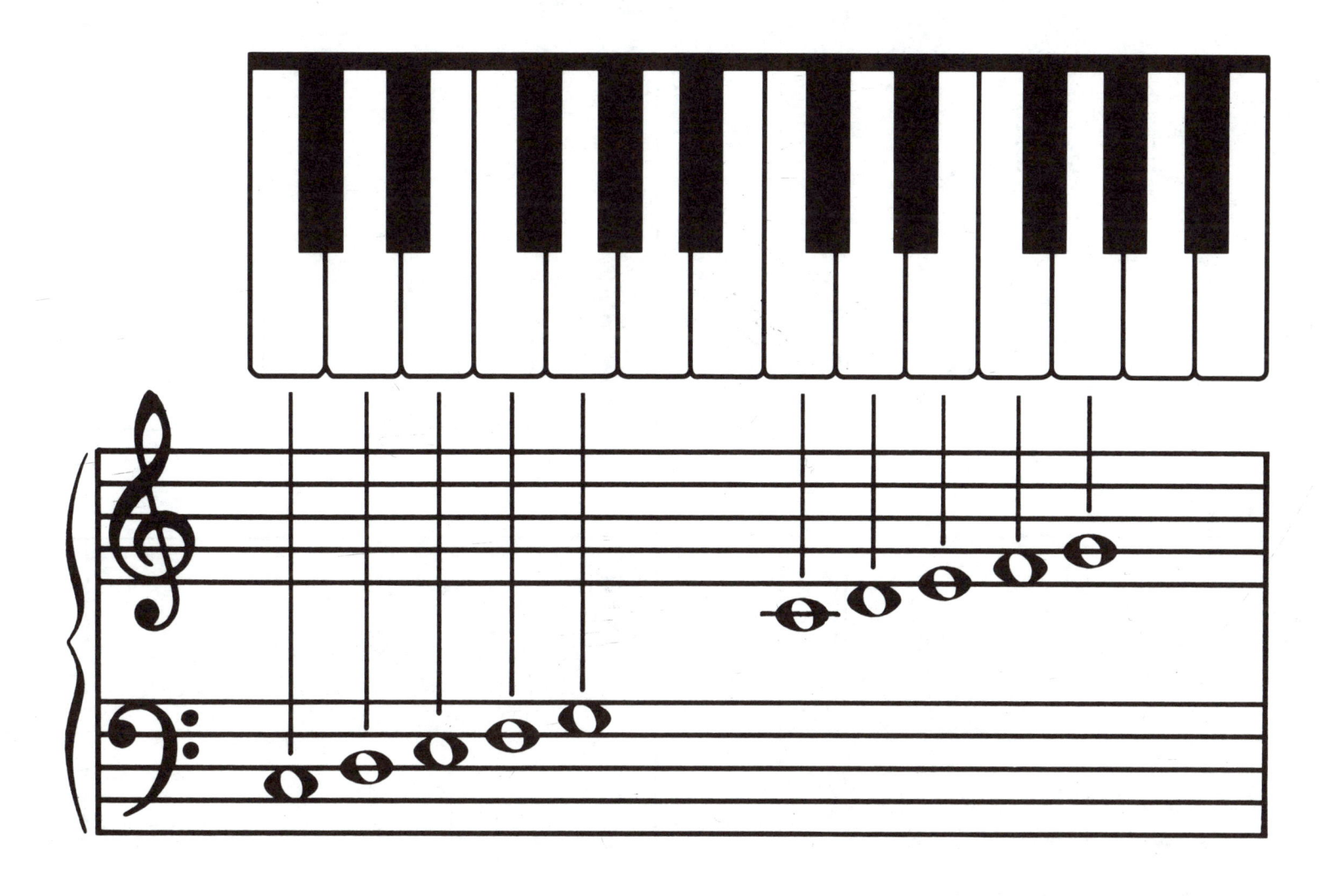

Use with page 41.

40

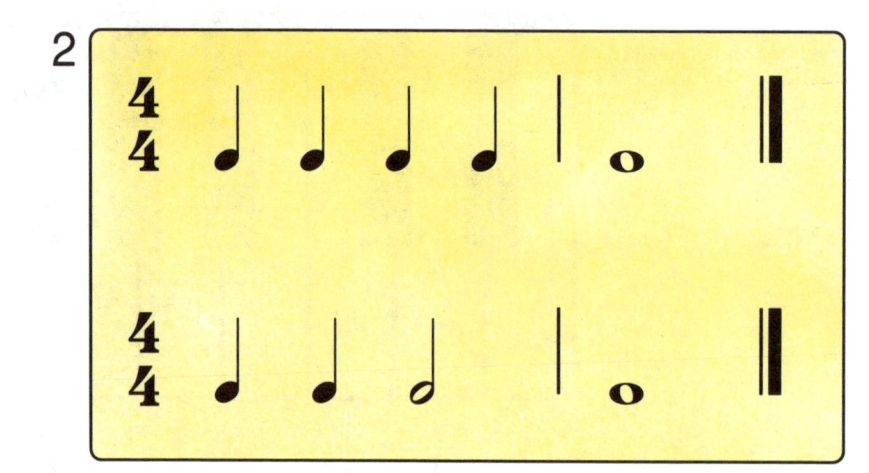

Use with page 42.

Rhythm Patterns

Your teacher will clap a rhythm pattern.
Circle the pattern that you hear.

41

Use with page 43.

Note Stem Direction

1. Color the notes with STEMS POINTING UP **pink**.
2. Color the notes with STEMS POINTING DOWN **green**.
3. Write the name under each note.

42

Use with page 44.

C Position

1. Color the areas containing a C **green**.
2. Color the areas containing a D **yellow**.
3. Color the areas containing an E **brown**.
4. Color the areas containing an F **purple**.
5. Color the areas containing a G **blue**.

43

Use with page 45.

Rhythm Patterns

Your teacher will clap a rhythm pattern.
Write the pattern that you hear.

1

Pattern: _____

2

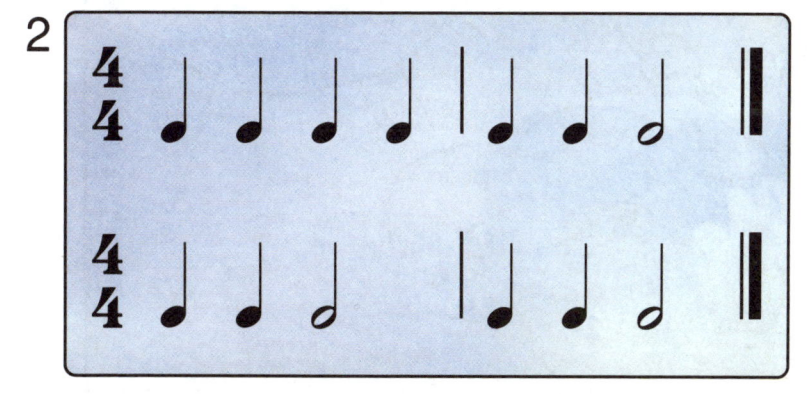

Pattern: _____

3

Pattern: _____

TEACHER: See page 48.

Review

1. Color the areas containing a C **gray**.
2. Color the areas containing a D **blue**.
3. Color the areas containing an E **brown**.
4. Color the areas containing an F **yellow**.
5. Color the areas containing a G **pink**.
6. Color the areas containing a TREBLE CLEF **orange**.
7. Color the areas containing a BASS CLEF **purple**.
8. Color the areas containing a *forte* (*f*) **green**.
9. Color the areas containing a *piano* (*p*) **black**.
10. Color the areas containing a *mezzo forte* (*mf*) **red**.

Use with pages 46–47.

Teacher's Examples

Page 5
(Play)

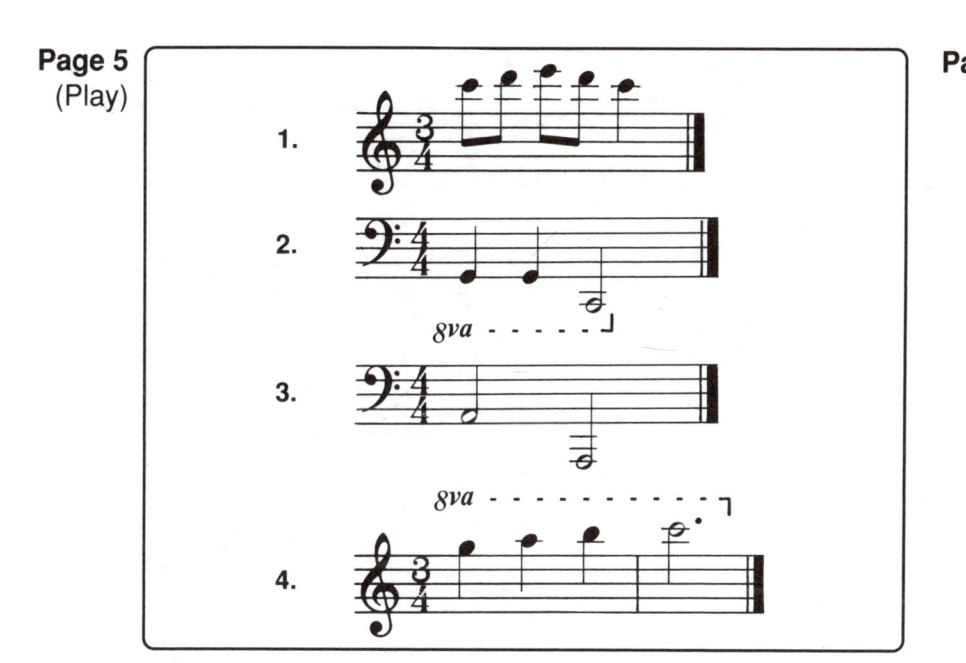

Page 10
(Clap)

Page 11
(Play)

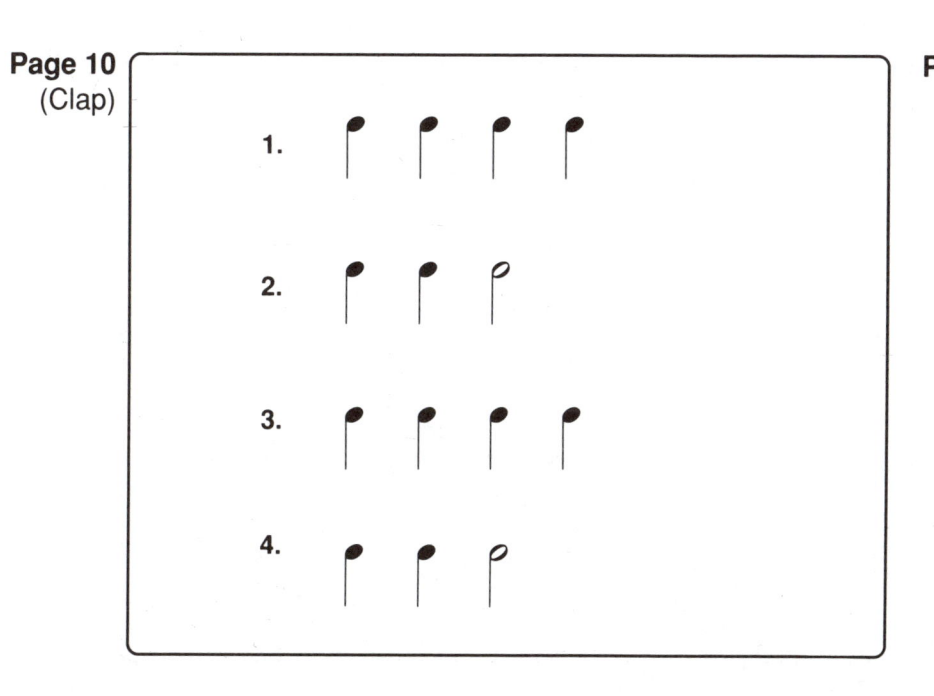

Page 14
(Play)

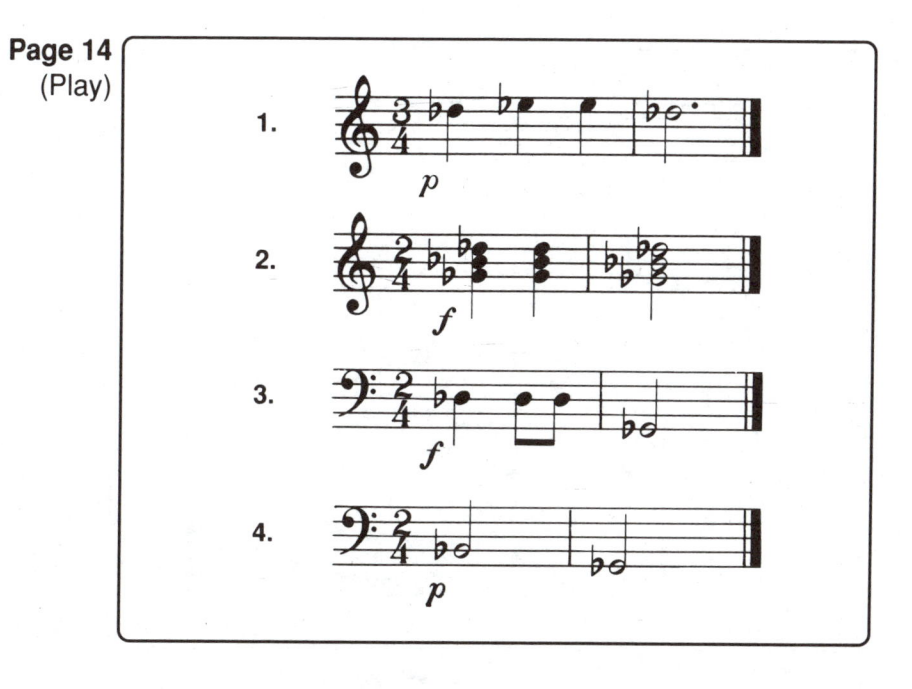

Teacher's Examples

Page 15
(Clap)

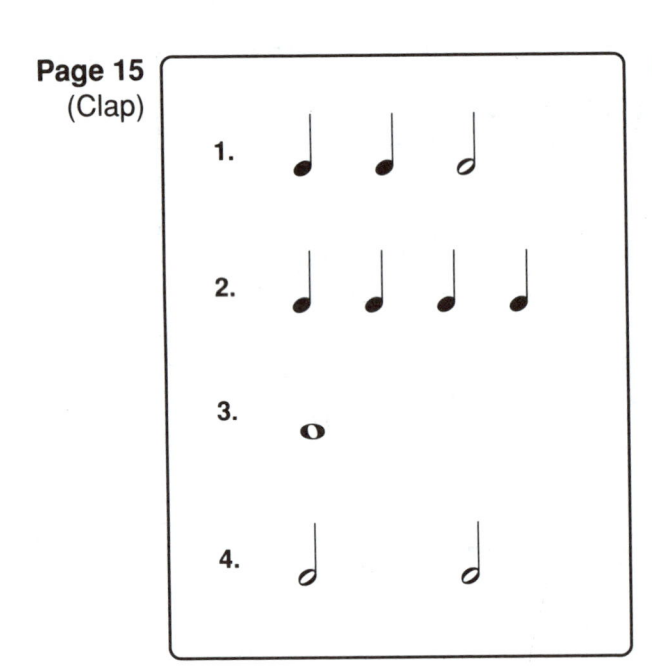

Page 18
(Play)

Page 20
(Play)

Page 16
(Play)

Page 22
(Clap)

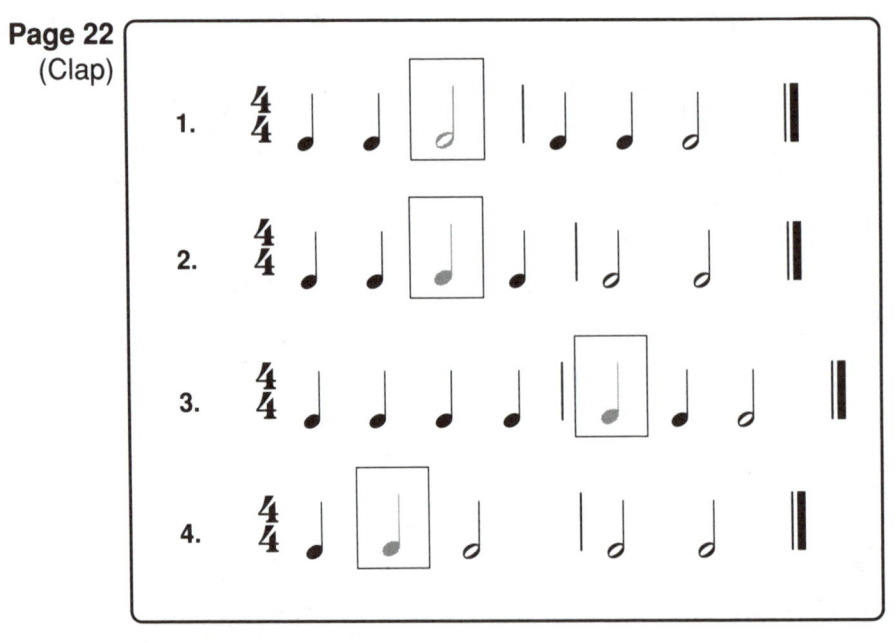

Teacher's Examples

Page 24
(Play)

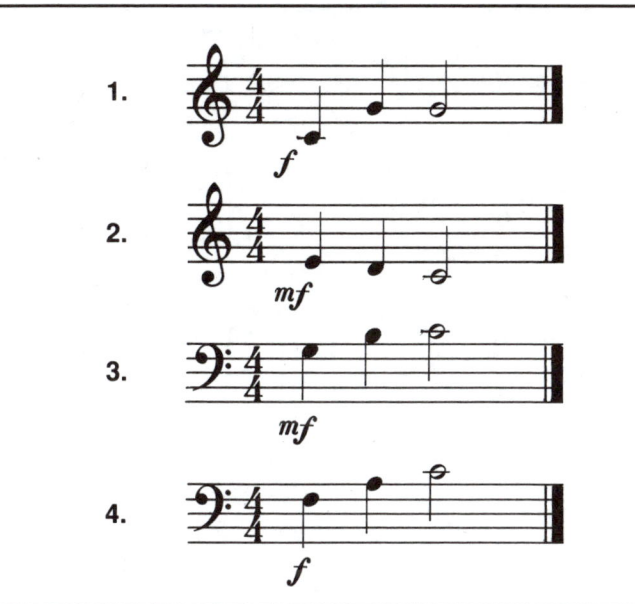

Page 26
(Clap)

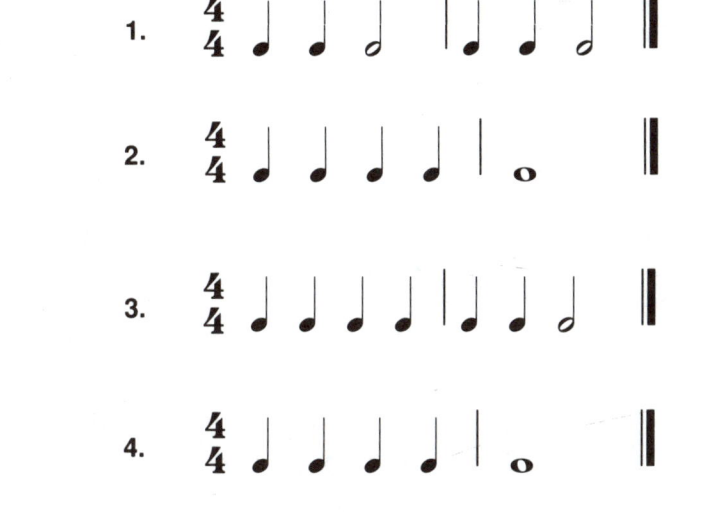

Page 28
(Clap)

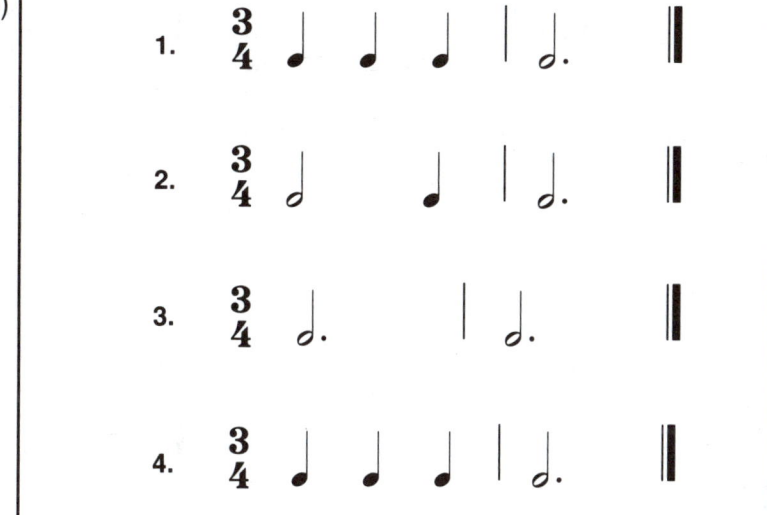

Page 31
(Play)

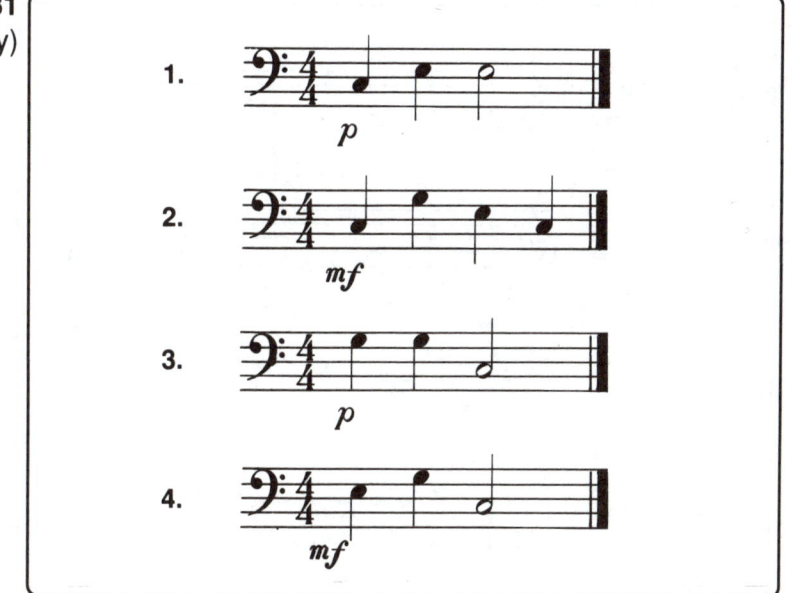

Teacher's Examples

Page 32
(Clap)

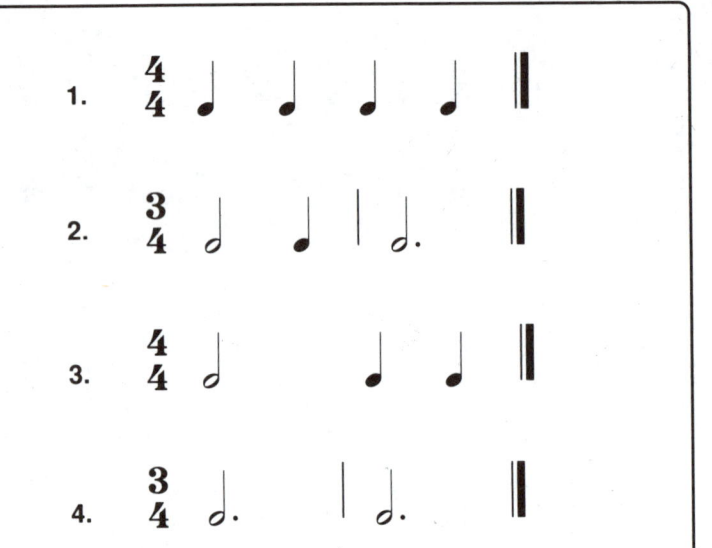

Page 36
(Play)

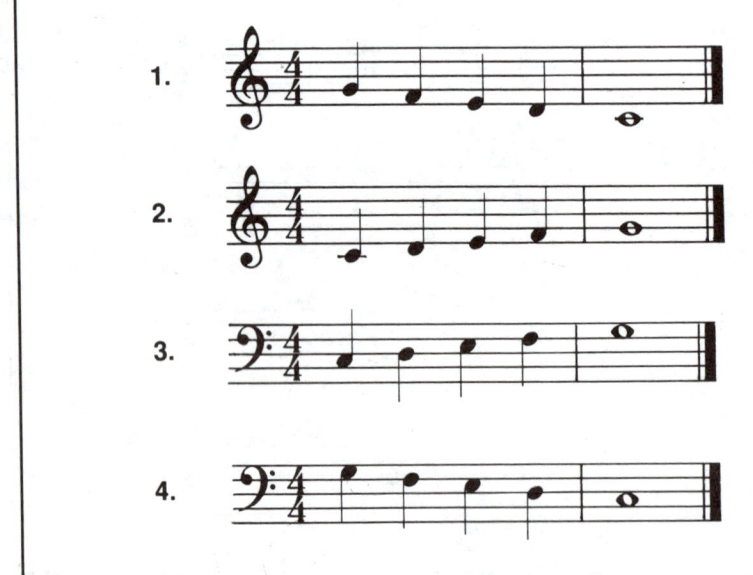

Page 40
(Clap)

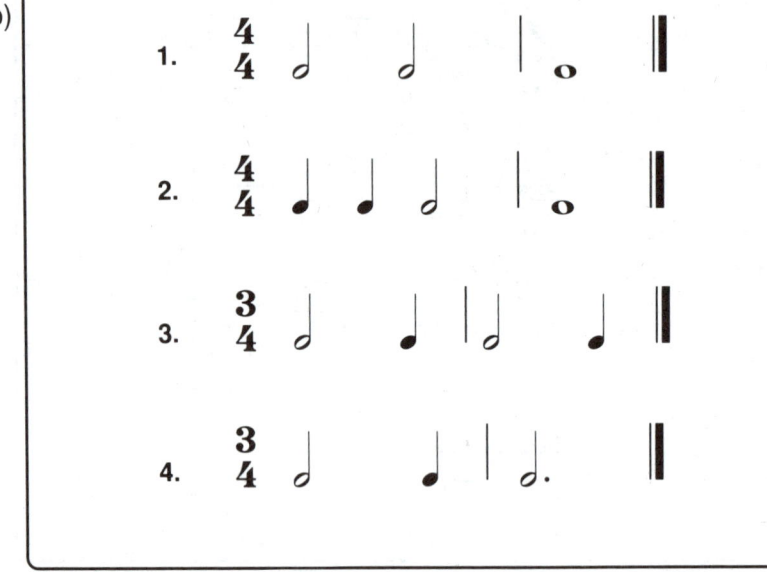

Page 43
(Clap)

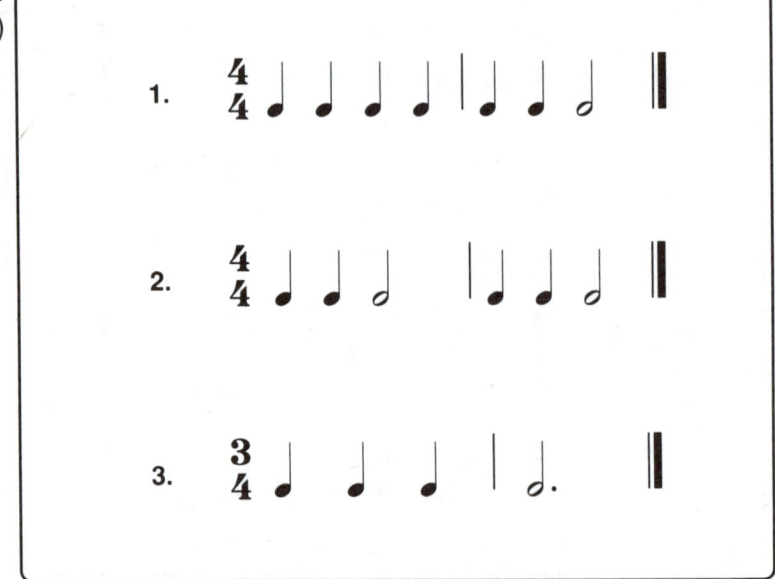